LIGHTNING
BOLT
BOOKS™

Experiment with a Plant's Living Environment

Nadia Higgins

Lerner Publications
Minneapolis

Lerner Publications Company
A division of Lerner Publishing Group, Inc.
241 First Avenue North
Minneapolis, MN 55401 USA

For reading levels and more information, look up this title at www.lernerbooks.com.

Library of Congress Cataloging-in-Publication Data

Higgins, Nadia.
    Experiment with a plant's living environment / by Nadia Higgins.
        pages   cm. — (Lightning Bolt Books™ — Plant Experiments)
    Includes index.
    ISBN 978-1-4677-5731-7 (lib. bdg. : alk. paper)
    ISBN 978-1-4677-6072-0 (pbk.)
    ISBN 978-1-4677-6242-7 (EB pdf)
    1. Plants—Experiments—Juvenile literature. I. Title. II. Series: Lightning bolt books.
    Plant experiments.
    QK52.6.H54 2015
    5580.78—dc23   2014020915

Manufactured in the United States of America
1 — BP — 12/31/14

Table of Contents

How Does Temperature Affect Seeds?

Summer's heat turns your tomatoes red over time.

You water tomato seeds, and they sprout. Sunlight makes them grow. Hungry caterpillars eat some of the plants, but the rest shoot up in the rich soil.

Gardeners help seedlings grow by watering them.

Your tomato plants change with their environment. A plant's environment includes nonliving things, such as soil, water, heat, and light. Living things, such as bugs and gardeners, also play a role.

Sunshine and warm weather help plants grow.

Spring's arrival is a major event for many plants. The long, warm days turn the whole world green again. Let's see what happens to sunflower seeds when spring's warmth arrives.

What you need:

three clear jars

tape

water

marker

thirty sunflower seeds

Steps:

1. Add very cold water to the first jar. Add room temperature water to the second jar. With an adult's help, add boiling water to the third jar.

2. Label the jars using the marker and the tape. Put ten seeds in each jar.

Label your jars "Cold," "Room Temp," and "Hot."

3. Put your jars in a spot with little light.

4. Check your jars twice a day for the next three days. Replace the hot, cold, and room temperature water in the jars each time you check them.

5. After three days, count how many seeds sprouted in each jar.

Which jar sprouted the most seeds?

Think It Through

Seeds sprout when the conditions are right. For most seeds, that means two main things: water and warmth. In cold places, gardeners plant seeds in spring when the ground is warm enough. Spring rains bring water.

How Do Worms Help Plants?

Animals would die without plants. Plants give off oxygen that animals breathe. Plants also provide food for animals.

Grasses provide food for this elephant.

Animals are part of a plant's living environment. Some animals help plants.

Bees help plants. They spread pollen from flower to flower so plants can make seeds.

Let's find out why earthworms are known as gardeners' best friends.

What you need:

nylon stocking

water

jar

camera

toilet paper roll

rubber band

garden soil (not potting soil)

shovel

ten worms

Steps:

1. Sprinkle the soil with water to make it moist. Add the worms to the soil. Then carefully scoop the soil and the worms into the jar with the shovel.

2. Put the toilet paper roll in the jar. Stretch the nylon stocking over the jar's mouth. Hold it in place with the rubber band.

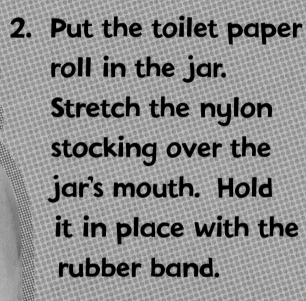

The toilet paper roll should stand upright inside the jar.

3. Put your jar someplace where it's not too bright. Next, take a picture of it.

4. Check your worms over the next two days.

In what direction are the worm trails moving?

5. Compare the jar to the picture you took.

When you're done with this experiment, dump the soil and the worms outside in a yard or garden.

Think It Through

The worms' wriggly bodies made tunnels. The tunnels help keep the soil loose. Roots can grow in these spaces more easily. Spaces in soil let in air that roots need. Those spaces can also hold water, so the soil stays moist.

How Does Oil Affect Plants?

Humans play an important part in a plant's environment. Think of the ways people help plants. We plant seeds. We turn on sprinklers, and we get rid of pests. But human activity can also hurt plants, even when people don't mean any harm.

Think of some of the ways people help and harm plants.

Smoke from factories and other kinds of pollution can kill plants. Sometimes ships carrying oil have accidents. Globs of thick, black oil leak into the water, harming plants onshore.

Underwater plants are often the first living things to be harmed by oil spills.

An experiment with cooking oil shows you how oil spills can harm plants. Let's give it a try.

What you need:

vegetable oil

water

two plates

two lettuce leaves

food brush

Steps:

1. Put one lettuce leaf on each plate.

Make sure your lettuce leaves are crisp and dry before coating them.

2. Use the brush to coat one leaf in water.

3. Then brush the second leaf with oil.

100% Pure
Vegetable Oil

4. Observe your leaves several times over the next hour.

What's happening to the lettuce leaves?

Think It Through

Lettuce leaves are covered in a waxy coating. Water beads up on the surface, but not oil. Oil flows into tiny holes on the surface of the leaf. The oil seeps inside, making the leaf wilt.

Salad dressing is often full of oil. Chefs dress their salads at the last minute to help keep the lettuce crisp.

21

How Does a Cactus Survive in the Desert?

From forests to deserts, plants live in all kinds of places. Often you can tell where a plant is from by how it looks or grows. The plant has special features that help it survive in its environment.

Ferns grow well in a forest's shade.

Compare a cactus to a leafy green plant. The cactus is covered in prickly spines. The cactus stem is a lot fatter too.

Plants in areas with cold weather often grow in clumps. They protect one another from icy winds.

How might these special features help the cactus live in the dry desert? Let's find out.

What you need:

kitchen scale

two large plastic bags

leafy green plant in a pot with soil

small cactus in a pot with soil

tape

pencil and paper

water

Steps:

1. Water both plants until the soil is moist.

2. Put a plastic bag around each pot. Seal the bags with tape at the base.

3. Weigh each pot, and record your results. Then put the pots in a warm, sunny spot.

The plastic bag keeps the moisture from escaping the plant's roots.

4. For the next week, weigh your plants daily and write down the numbers.

5. Organize your data into a line graph, with one line for each plant. Compare your graphs.

The lines on both graphs go down. But they go down faster on the leafy plant's graph.

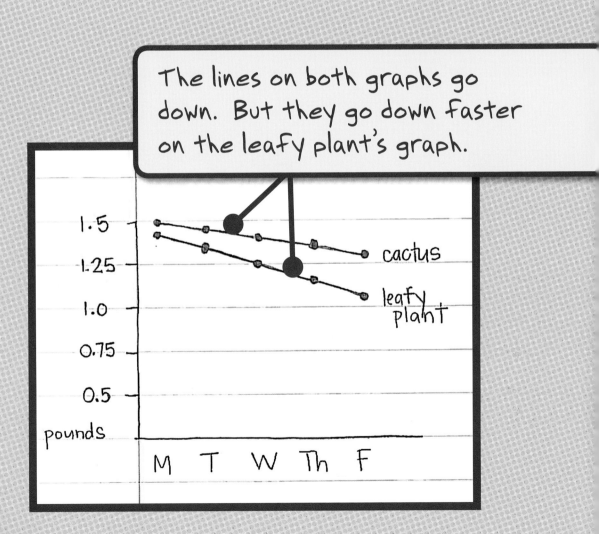

Think It Through

Both plants lost weight. Water vapor left through airholes on the surface. The green plant lost a great deal of water through its leaves. Without leaves, the cactus kept more water.

The cactus stores water in its fat, waxy stem.

Report Like a Scientist

Make your next science report a winner by showing the five science steps.

1. Ask a question. What do you want to find out?

2. Describe your research. What facts did you discover before you did your experiment?

3. Tell your hypothesis. What did you think your experiment would show?

4. Describe your experiment. Tell what materials you used and what steps you took.

5. Draw a conclusion. Does your data support your hypothesis?

Fun Facts

- One tablespoon of soil holds around 50 billion microscopic creatures. Those creatures loosen the soil and make it rich with nutrients.

- A "living rock" is a desert plant that stores water in its roots. This grayish plant looks like a rock, so animals just pass it by.

- About four hundred thousand known plants grow on Earth. They grow in every kind of environment.

- Plants give off oxygen that we need to breathe. One large tree can provide enough oxygen for two people.

- A young sunflower follows the sun's path across the sky each day. In the morning, the plant's flower head faces east. By night, it faces west.

Glossary

environment: a plant's surroundings, including both living and nonliving things

oxygen: a gas in the air that animals and people need to breathe

pollution: the presence of substances that make soil, water, and air harmful to living things

root: a plant part that takes in water and minerals

water vapor: water in the form of gas

Further Reading

Blue Planet Biomes: Plants
http://www.blueplanetbiomes
.org/plants.htm

Flounders, Anne. *Growing Good Food.*
South Egremont, MA: Red Chair Press, 2014.

Missouri Botanical Garden: Plant Adaptations
http://www.mbgnet.net/bioplants/adapt.html

Science Buddies: Plant Biology Project Ideas
http://www.sciencebuddies.org/science-fair-projects
/search.shtml?v=ia&ia=PlantBio

Taylor-Butler, Christine. *Experiments with Plants.*
New York: Children's Press, 2012.

US Forest Service: Celebrating Wildflowers
http://www.fs.fed.us/wildflowers/kids/index.shtml

Index

Photo Acknowledgments

The images in this book are used with the permission of: © Rick Orndorf, pp. 2, 7, 8, 9, 12, 13, 14, 18, 19, 20, 24, 25, 27; © base1101658/Shutterstock Images, p. 4; © Humannet/ Shutterstock Images, p. 5; © iravgustin/Shutterstock Images, p. 6; © Kryvenok Anastasiia/Shutterstock Images, p. 10; © Ikordela/Shutterstock Images, p. 11; © zD. Kucharski K. Kucharska/Shutterstock Images, p. 15; © Subin Pumsom/Shutterstock Images, p. 16; © Foto Osmeh/Shutterstock Images, p. 17; © Nitr/Shutterstock Images, p. 21; © Jon Bilous/Shutterstock Images, p. 22; © Jason Patrick Ross/Shutterstock Images, p. 23; © Red Line Editorial, p. 26; © michaeljung/Shutterstock Images, p. 28; © Madlen/Shutterstock Images, p. 30; © Brooke Becker/Shutterstock Images, p. 31.

Front cover: © iStockphoto.com/ravipatchan.

Main body text set in Johann Light 30/36.